THE FAITH WITHIN

Healing After Stillbirth, Miscarriage, or Loss of a Baby

SHANEASE RUSSELL

CONTENTS

Foreword	vii
1. My Story	1
2. You Are Not Alone	15
3. Healing in the Process	23
4. Walking Through Grief *Don't Blame Yourself, but Educate Yourself*	33
5. Prioritize Your Health	51
6. Don't Be Afraid to Share Your Story	59
7. Restoration	65
8. The Aftermath	75
9. Having the Faith to Move Forward	79
Special Message	85
10. God is My Strength	87
Acknowledgments	101
About the Author	103
References	105

THE FAITH WITHIN

Copyright © 2021 by Shanease Russell

Published by Chic Rose LLC. www.shanease.com

All rights reserved. No part of this publication may be reproduced or used in any form without written permission from the publisher, except in the case of brief quotations embodied in critical articles and reviews.

Scripture quotations marked NIV are taken from the Holy Bible, New International Version®, NIV®. Copyright © 1973, 1978, 1984, 2011 by Biblica, Inc. Used by permission. All rights reserved worldwide. Scripture quotations marked NLT are taken from the Holy Bible, New Living Translation, Copyright © 1996, 2004, 2007 by Tyndale House Foundation. Used by permission of Tyndale House Publishers, Inc., Carol Stream, Illinois 60188. All rights reserved. Scripture quotations marked KJV are taken from the Holy Bible, King James Version. Scripture quotations marked NKJV are taken from the New King James Version®. Copyright © 1982 by Thomas Nelson. Used by permission. All rights reserved.

Cover Design by Jennifer Stimson

Hardcover ISBN: 979-8-9851197-0-1

Paperback ISBN: 979-8-9851197-2-5

Ebook ISBN: 979-8-9851197-1-8

Audiobook ISBN: 979-8-9851197-3-2

Printed in the United States of America. First Edition, 2021

1 2 3 4 5 6 7 8 9 10

DEDICATION

This book is dedicated to my mother, Francis Teresa Ray, my grandmother, Betty Ann Ray and my daughter, Gia Teresa Russell. Until we met again in heaven.

FOREWORD

A well known quote by Mahatma Gandhi states, "Be the change that you wish to see in the world". It has always been my mission as a board certified obstetrician gynecologist to care for women and to be the change in medicine that I wanted to see in the world. More importantly, it has been my desire to be the change that I wanted to see in the field of women's health. I have practiced in the city of Atlanta, Georgia for over 20 years and have been able to take care of many patients throughout my years as a physician. There are some relationships that grow into a lasting relationship almost like friendships from the doctor patient relationships I have been blessed to have.

There are some patients that you meet in your

practice that are unforgettable. I met Shanease Russell when she was 25 years old and found her to be a very special person who has become near and dear to my heart over the past several years. I met her at a pivotal stage in her adult life. I found myself attracted to the strength that she possesses. I knew that she was a kind and beautiful spirit within the first minutes of meeting her. I was drawn to Shanease through an interesting diagnosis that resonated with me. There was also a connection through her family history and, from that moment on, she has left an imprint on my heart. She's always referred to me as though I was a physician/mother figure to her and, despite what she experienced, her strength has remained immeasurable.

It has been said that bad things happen to good people. With the trials and tribulations that Shanease Russell has experienced, this has more than qualified her to share her life through the pages of this book. What I like about her book is that she is vulnerable and honest with her story. She has had experiences that she is brave enough to share and that I know many women and others could benefit from after reading this book. From being a humble spirit to a strong warrior, she has handled some of the most challenging times a woman can face with grace and power. She is a God fearing woman who reminded me of how I very well may have handled some of the life situations that she experienced. The key to handling these experiences is to know that pain is your purpose. As Shanease states, "Too often we mistake our pain as the ultimate purpose God has for our lives". Don't let your pain determine your purpose, try to allow God and your struggle to give you strength.

—Jacqueline M. Walters, MD

Chapter One
MY STORY

My husband and I met at Georgia State University during the Summer of 2018. It was my junior year of college. I vividly remember we had a class together —Business Communications and Public Speaking. One of the requirements in this class was to give a speech every month or so. I remember when my husband (before I knew who he was) got up and spoke before our class. He had an all-black suit on. I thought to myself, "Umm-hmm, who is that?" He was so well-spoken and commanded the room when he presented. Mind you, I was super shy and did not like giving speeches. On the last day of class, before our final exam, I remember I wasted some water from my water bottle on my desk. He happened to be sitting next to me and said, "Let me help you with that." Before final exams started, which was shortly after the incident with the water, he asked me for my cell phone number. Looking back, I think it would have been incredibly awkward for me to see him—being super shy—after the water incident. Fortunately, that was not the case because I gave him my number, and the rest is history.

Fast forward a few years, and we are now engaged. I was twenty-five-years old and filled with excitement as I would soon be marrying the man God hand-picked and destined for me. We were excited to share the news with our families and friends. A month or so after our engagement, I had my regular annual appointment with my OBGYN, including my annual pap smear. During this appointment, my doctor felt something unusual during my vaginal examination and immediately requested an MRI to further investigate. When the MRI images became available for my viewing, via my patient portal, I remember being nervous to even look at the MRI images, but once the images popped up on my computer, I was in total shock when my eyes met the fibroid, the size of a small cantaloupe, which had taken up residence in my uterus. I was devastated—to say the least. Immediately, fear set in, my mind began racing with all sorts of questions, and I wondered, "God, why me? I just got engaged to the man whom you chose for me. Is this going to impact my ability to have children?" I recalled my family history. My mother passed away from breast cancer at a young age. She was diagnosed with breast cancer around twenty-six and passed away at the tender young age of twenty-eight. I thought, "Oh my God, what if this fibroid tumor is cancerous?" At the time, I did not have any answers to these questions. All I could do was pray that I would be healed through the process. When I initially found out, I was a bit down and began to notice that my clothes and my stomach would stick out some. I had a slim figure, but knowing that I had this fibroid, I became self-conscious of how my clothes fit. I really did not know much about fibroids before that day. I had vaguely heard television commercials about fibroids. I immediately began my research on fibroids. What are fibroids? What caused fibroids? Are they genetic? Was there a relationship between fibroids and breast cancer? How common were fibroids? During this time, I began to have brief conversations with family, friends, and co-workers. These brief conversations helped me understand that my fibroid issue was more common than I knew. I was blessed to have a close family member who is a medical doctor with over twenty years of experience, Dr. Marilyn Carter. I was able to speak to her, send her the MRI images, and get a better understanding of fibroids. Her support extended beyond her medical expertise. She was also very supportive by praying for me, encouraging me, and sharing scriptures to reference, from the bible, to pray for healing.

Based on my research, I revealed alarming statistics surrounding black women and fibroids. "Nearly a quarter of black women between 18 and 30 have fibroids compared to about 6% of white women, according to some national estimates. By age 35, that number increases to 60%. Black women are also two to three times more likely to have recurring fibroids or suffer from complications."[1]

Not only was I curious about researching the medical aspect of fibroids, but I was also curious about researching the spiritual cause of fibroids. I truly believe that our thoughts and mindset can impact our bodies. I began to further my research by looking for more holistic medical approaches for the root cause of fibroids. According to Ayurvedic Practitioners, "Ayuseva," the uterus is considered to be the vessel that is the holder of a woman's creative power the power that she uses to create, nurture, and sustain a child, as well as to consciously create her own life and thus fulfill her life-purpose. A woman's menstrual cycle allows her to tangibly connect to her creative power on a monthly basis. Overall, this source recommended that the essential aspects of healing fibroids holistically support a woman to acknowledge and process her emotions and completely address any unresolved past experiences with her mother or other significant women in her life. Also, focus on supporting self-discovery as a woman so that she can fully embrace her creative power and that of her cycle to develop a sense of fulfillment and purpose in her life. In addition to the mental or spiritual aspect, diet can also impact the likelihood of developing fibroids. I would find that uterine fibroids can be caused by excessive mental stress, long-term emotional suppression, lack of exercise, and the consumption of junk food including: wheat, refined sugars, and excess dairy.[2]

My physician's advice was to have a "myomectomy" to remove the fibroid tumor. Within a month or so, post fibroid diagnosis, I was scheduled for the surgical procedure to remove the fibroid. The day of surgery, a plethora of emotions attacked me mentally. I was nervous and scared out of my mind. I remember my family, fiancé, and his mother being there to support me. In the end, the surgery was a huge success, and the fibroid was not cancerous. Praise God!

It took about six weeks to heal from the surgery. After healing from the surgery and returning to normalcy, my fiancé and I were able to plan our wedding. In the back of my mind, I still had feelings of fear. My fiancé and I would constantly talk about the fibroid journey because we knew we wanted to try to have a child very early in our marriage. In retrospect, I wish I had not let my fears of not being able to conceive remain at the forefront of my mind and the topic of my and my fiancé's conversations as we found out a month after our honeymoon we were expecting! We were so excited and nervous—yet so grateful to God that we were able to get pregnant. Many people questioned our decision to get pregnant so soon, but they had no idea of our journey before getting pregnant or my medical history. Our parents were very excited as this would be the first grandchild for both my parents and my husband's parents. Our baby was going to be so loved and spoiled. As time passed, we found out that we were having a baby girl. I immediately began to shop for all the cute, pretty, and pink onesies, hair bows, and accessories. It seems like a week did not go by when I was not shopping for our baby girl and dreaming about what her personality would be like. I would also daydream about how I would one day take her to ballet lessons, have tea parties, and play dress-up. All of the things a new mother may think about when expecting a baby girl.

My in-laws would come by our house on the weekends to help us prepare and begin to set up the nursery for our baby girl. We had a chandelier installed in her room ceiling, all white, custom furniture, and a luxurious tufted white crib. I vividly remember shopping with my family at Pottery Barn Baby, picking out the soft gray colored rocking chair and ottoman, and strategically placing beautiful, sheer, white butterflies on the baby's room wall—on one side of her dresser mirror.

As I advanced through my pregnancy, I planned and scheduled my maternity photoshoot at the Cator Woolford Gardens. This garden features over thirty-nine acres of martyrs woods, including a beautiful garden that captures the 1920s historic styled architecture and southern charm. This is one of the greatest memories of my pregnancy, and the weather that day was perfect. We took pictures in the garden, and I remember there were so many butterflies in the garden that day, and an orange butterfly landed near my belly. It was important to me to have maternity photos commemorating our pregnancy journey. I felt it was essential to capture the joy and anticipation of our baby girl. I was excited to take the photos because I was nearing the end of my second trimester, and I felt it was the perfect time to take photos before I reached the "uncomfortable phase of pregnancy." The day of my photoshoot was electrifying and a joyous occasion. I was pampered, had my makeup applied professionally, and to finally step into my beautiful blush pink custom gown, and floral handmade headband made the day perfect. The photographer we hired was the same photographer whom we used for our wedding, so it was special for her to capture this next milestone in our lives as well. The photographer left no stone unturned. She laid out the red carpet for me. She literally had a "diva fan" in the middle of the garden to create a dramatic wind effect for the extremely long train on the dress to softly and mystically flow in the air with the wind. It was simply beautiful! My little sisters and aunt were present and helping while we prepped for the photoshoot and strolled through the mystical gardens. I wore all pink that day so that once the pictures were shared with family and friends, the gender of our bundle of joy—a baby girl—would finally be revealed without one word being whispered. I will never forget that day and moment in my life.

After a few weeks went by, I was approximately around the 30th-week mark of my pregnancy. I had recently been showered with two baby showers and was feeling so overjoyed with all of the love, gifts, and cards I received from my family and friends for our baby girl. Later that month, I had a checkup appointment with my OBGYN. On the day of my appointment, my blood pressure was slightly elevated, and based on other symptoms, my OBGYN immediately referred me to a perinatal specialist. At this point, I was around 34 weeks pregnant. I just vaguely remember the specialist advising me that I would be seeing them twice a week to monitor the baby. On the same day, I was diagnosed with preeclampsia. Prior to my pregnancy, I did not know what preeclampsia was.

According to the Preeclampsia Foundation, "preeclampsia is a condition unique to human pregnancy. It is diagnosed by the elevation of the expectant mother's blood pressure, usually after the 20th week of pregnancy. Most women with preeclampsia will deliver healthy babies and fully recover. However, some women will experience complications, several of which may be life-threatening to the mother and/or baby. A woman's condition can progress to severe preeclampsia very quickly. The rate of preeclampsia in the United States has increased by 25% in the last two decades and is a leading cause of maternal and infant illness and death."[3]

It was a Sunday night, and I recall just feeling like the baby wasn't moving as much. I decided to take a shower to see if that would stimulate movement. I went to lie down after my shower. Lying in my bed, the room felt dark, quiet, and something just didn't feel right in my spirit. I got up, went to the restroom, and immediately saw a pool of blood in the toilet. I screamed for my husband to call 911. I could hear my husband speaking with the 911 specialist in the background, and everything began to move so quickly. "How many weeks is your wife?" Is she breathing?" "Do not flush the toilet." I vaguely remember calling my mother-in-law in shock. I also quickly texted my cousin, Dr. Marylin, to pray for me. Next thing I knew, there were paramedics upstairs in my home, putting me on a stretcher to be carried down the steps. While I was on the stretcher, being carried downstairs by the paramedics, I recall seeing my brother-in-law and sister-in-law, who rushed to our home after being advised by my mother-in-law of the circumstances. They lived close by at the time, less than five minutes away from our house, and were able to rush to our house rather quickly. I remember being carried out of my house by the paramedics, and once we were outside, it was raining. I felt the rain on my body—cold. I was shaking, shivering, and afraid. The paramedic put me in the ambulance and placed an oxygen mask over my face. I just remember her trying to keep me awake by talking to me and asking questions. "Are you okay?" "Hang in there. We are almost there." I felt my eyes getting heavier and heavier, but I was fighting to stay awake, and at the same time praying for my baby. "Lord save my baby."

Once we made it inside the hospital and into an exam room, I remember not hearing my baby's heartbeat—after arriving at the hospital and the doctors placing me on the fetal monitor. At that moment I feared that my baby girl did not make it, but I still had hope. The next thing I recall, I was being rushed in for an emergency C-section. I just remember a huge bright light over the operating table. An oxygen mask was placed over my face, and within a few minutes, I was asleep.

After waking up, I remember the room being very dark, and I vaguely remember speaking briefly with my husband. The next thing I noticed after waking up was my dad and aunt were near my side. There was a needle in my arm because I needed a blood transfusion. I didn't realize it at the time, but I had lost so much blood that I could have died. I kept asking how is the baby? Is she okay? And they kept saying to just worry about me, make sure you're okay. The baby will be fine. In my mind I knew something was terribly wrong but I didn't ask any more questions. Suddenly, the doctor came into the room. Oddly enough, his face looked familiar, and I recalled that he was the father of one of my debutante group members from high school. He told us the baby was stillborn, but they resuscitated her, and she had lost a lot of oxygen to her brain. I was devastated, destroyed, and I didn't know what to do but just pray. Later, I remember being in the room, and my husband and I had some time to ourselves to process everything. I was still kind of out of it because of the pain medication. I was not able to see my baby. I could only see pictures of her at first in the Newborn Intensive Care Unit (NICU) that my family had taken on their phones. Imagine not being able to hold or see your baby. I was so overwhelmed seeing the pictures of the IVs and tubes connected to her little body. There were so many tubes connected to her, I could not count them. I felt helpless and would have done anything to make her whole, healthy, and safe. That night in the hospital, I just cried and prayed. I called some of my prayer warrior family members who lived in South Georgia, and we prayed on the phone. I begged God to heal my baby. I pleaded and cried in the Holy Spirit. I was so destroyed. That was one of the lowest points in my life I had ever experienced. After several hours passed, my husband and I talked to the doctors and based on how much oxygen she lost to the brain, there was little hope that she would survive. The nurses prepared time for me and transported me to the NICU to see my baby. I was transported in the hospital bed because I could not stand up. The first time I saw my husband cry was in that moment—the moment we both saw our baby girl. My heart was broken. There was nothing I could do to heal my baby and there was no physical way for me to wipe the tears that were rolling down my husband's face. I watched each teardrop, one by one as I laid "unwillingly" in the hospital bed. We had some time with our baby, and I was able to hold her. The chaplain from the hospital came and prayed with us. My grandparents, father, family members, and in-laws were near our side. My husband held our baby girl, Gia Teresa Russell, until she took her last breath. No pain can compare to the heart-wrenching pain of losing your baby, watching her die, and there is nothing you can do to save her. I would have given my life to save her life.

Chapter Two

YOU ARE NOT ALONE

I **feel that losing** a baby is one of most difficult and painful experiences in life. If you have suffered a recent loss of an infant or know someone who has been impacted by such a loss, let me first acknowledge your loss. I have tremendous empathy and sorrow for anyone who experienced this type of devastating loss and pain. It may seem hard now, but trust in God and know that there is a purpose for everything happening in your life. The Word tells us, "And we know that in all things God works for the good of those who love him, who have been called according to his purpose" (Romans 8:28 NIV).

But most importantly, I want you to know that "you are not alone." Often times women feel alone after having suffered from a loss of a baby, whether it be from a miscarriage, stillbirth, or Sudden Infant Death Syndrome (SIDS). I stress it again, please know that you are NOT alone. What inspired me to write this book is after my husband and I faced the loss of our baby—stillbirth—I received an abundance of encouragement and love from other women pouring into me who experienced a similar loss as well. Women from my job shared their stories with me who I would have never imagined suffered such a loss. Also, there were women from my church that comforted and encouraged me and shared their stories of when their daughters, themselves, or close relatives experienced the loss of a baby. There were also women in my extended family who shared their stories that I had not even known about regarding miscarriage and stillbirth. All of their stories and transparency inspired me to write this book, but it also highlighted—sadly, how I feel women endure so much and often we don't open up about our pain and suffering. Personally, I felt afraid to share my story. Afraid others would judge me, talk about me, and look down on me. I also feared that no one quite understood what I was going through. I felt ashamed, and I also questioned what was wrong with my body, but most of all, in the beginning, I felt alone.

My prayer is that this book will silence the shame of pregnancy loss and inspire other women to encourage others and share their stories.

I feel that women often share the glamorous side of pregnancy but don't often share some of the unflattering realities of pregnancy, the loss of a child, and the aftermath. In a world driven by social media, we often see women sharing their maternity pictures with their glowing skin and perfectly round baby bump. In general, on social media, I feel that women tend to highlight the positive moments, especially on Instagram and Facebook, and people can curate a "cookie-cutter" portfolio of positive images.

Subconsciously, we can tend to compare our lives with the lives of our peers or our social network. I remember after getting married in March of 2018, I was happy to see some of my former classmates and friends getting married around the same time. In one instance, a couple of my classmates from college got married within a month after each other. It was often fun to connect with and share when you are at similar points in life. Likewise, when I became pregnant, it was exciting to see some of my classmates and even some celebrities that were due around the same time as I. It was so exciting to experience shopping for different maternity clothes, recognizing and embracing the new changes in my body. With social media, it was fun to see different people having gender reveal parties and all of the creative maternity shoots, baby shower and nursery ideas. I found myself making Pinterest boards filled with nursery ideas and cute baby outfits.

However, once my husband and I suffered the loss, it was important that I protected my thoughts and "guarded my heart." By guarding my heart, I did not want to become consumed with comparing myself to others on social media. It was easy for me to log in to Instagram and see other people who were pregnant or recently had babies. It was not that I was not happy for other people but more so a deep sorrow and sadness of the loss that my husband and I recently faced. Recent studies have shown that there is a link between social media and depression. According to the Journal of Social and Clinical Psychology, "What we found overall is that if you use less social media, you are actually less depressed and less lonely, meaning that the decreased social media use is what causes that qualitative shift in your well-being," said Jordyn Young, co-author of the paper and a senior at the University of Pennsylvania. If you have recently faced a loss of a pregnancy or suffered from a stillbirth, it may be helpful to take a small break from social media—if you can. It can become easy to harbor jealousy or comparative thoughts towards others when engulfed in social media. My personal suggestion is to focus on self-improvement and strengthening your relationship with God. I personally found that God was the one source who could heal my grief and pain. Through this book, my prayer is that you will grow spiritually and strengthen your relationship with God. I hope the tools I share that helped me to move forward after suffering the loss of my child will help you as well.

After suffering a miscarriage or stillbirth, some women tend to "shut down" and may try to hide or mask the pain they have experienced or are currently experiencing. By shutting down, we may feel alone and fail to realize that we are not alone. According to the Centers for Disease Control and Prevention (CDC), "each year about 24,000 babies are stillborn in the United States. Furthermore, about 31% of pregnancies confirmed after implantation end in miscarriage. Which is roughly one of every three pregnancies."[1] My prayer is that this book will help encourage someone and remove the stigma and shame of discussing healing after losing a baby.

It is important to know that your life has a purpose. What helped me heal and go through this process was knowing that whenever we suffer a loss in life, God has to allow it to happen. Anything that has happened where the devil tried to steal your joy or the enemy tried to attack you, God allowed it to happen. According to James 1:12 NIV, "Blessed is the one who perseveres under trial because, having stood the test, that person will receive the crown of life that the Lord has promised to those who love him." The way I think of it is, God trusted me and thought I was strong enough to handle this to allow me (and my husband) to go through the pain of losing our first child, but I remain in faith and know that God has a purpose for this pain. "Let us not become weary in doing good, for at the proper time we will reap a harvest if we do not give up" (Galatians 6:9 NIV).

I strongly believe that my purpose in going through this pain was to encourage and help other women heal who have been devastated by the loss of a baby. No matter the stage of your pregnancy or the age of your baby, as a mother, there was a strong bond between you and your baby. I remember when I heard her first heartbeats and felt her movements and kicks in my belly, I bonded instantly. No one or nothing can replace the love you and your child shared, but by having faith in God, He can help you be strong and heal through the pain. "Thou wilt keep him in perfect peace, whose mind is stayed on thee: because he trusteth in thee" (Isaiah 26 KJV).

So, I want to encourage you today to stay strong, keep your faith, and know that God will restore you! Just as God restored Sarah as she was barren in her later days, God can restore you. And God said to Abraham, "Regarding Sarai, your wife —her name will no longer be Sarai. From now on, her name will be Sarah. And I will bless her and give you a son from her! Yes, I will bless her richly, and she will become the mother of many nations. Kings of nations will be among her descendants" (Genesis 17:15-16 NLT). "It was by faith that even Sarah was able to have a child, though she was barren and was too old. She believed that God would keep his promise" (Hebrews 11:11 NLT). Sarah's story was so encouraging for me. Without a shadow of a doubt, I knew the same way God healed Sarah, the same way He could heal me. If God did it before, He could do it again! At first, and living in the moment, it proved to be very difficult, but it got a little better with each passing day. I tried thinking and focusing on the positives in my life. I would try to think and focus on the things I was grateful for. "Lord, if you allowed me to survive this, it must be for a purpose. I may not know it now, but I know '…that all things work together for the good of them who love God and are called according to His purpose.'" (Romans 8:28 KJV).

Chapter Three

HEALING IN THE PROCESS

Experiencing the loss of a baby is traumatic, and there are a lot of emotions that you experience, especially as a mother. For me, after facing the stillbirth of my daughter, many things easily triggered certain emotions. Going through pregnancy, one of the most exciting things you look forward to is your baby's pending "due date." And, as much as I looked forward to it, after having lost my baby at 34 weeks pregnant when my baby's actual due date came, that was one of the hardest days, through this process, for me. She was due on December 6, 2018, so when the day came, all I wanted to do was just lay in the bed. I encourage you to allow yourself to have time to grieve. Everyone's process is different, but for me, this was one of the hardest days. I remember calling on a family member and bonding with her to help with the healing process on that day—she, too, had suffered a stillbirth from her first pregnancy. She offered advice and encouragement to help me press forward.

There are so many common emotional triggers for those who have faced a miscarriage, stillbirth, or loss of an infant. Some of those for me, during the first few weeks of the loss, was when I would happen to go to the store, mall, or just out and would come across young babies or pregnant women. Your pain may be triggered by simply passing the baby section in a store or seeing or hearing certain baby commercials on television. I remember being in Target one day and simply passing by the baby aisle and not feeling the same. I would also see some of the items we had for our baby girl, like little onesies, and I would have to hold back my tears.

There are many emotions and stages of grief that you experience after going through your loss. Some of the immediate feelings may be shock and numbness. I remember after leaving the hospital and returning home just feeling heavy and weighted. I felt denial. I was thinking, "Did this really happen to us? Why God?" I was feeling powerless, defeated, and exhausted.

You may tend to immediately think of your baby, which is natural. Early on, I remember longing to hold my baby in my arms. I remember searching for answers—just feeling an overall loss of joy—feeling guilt and shame. For me, moments like these early on caused sadness after facing the loss. However, I would always try to stay strong in God's Word and not harbor any anger or jealousy when I think about the loss or see other babies. I know that what God has for me is for me, and I trusted that He would restore my joy just as He did! One of my favorite scriptures is Romans 8:28 KJV, "And we know that all things work together for good to them that love God, to them who are called according to his purpose." God always has the perfect plan.

I remember one of my aunts, who suffered from a stillbirth years ago, encouraging me. She told me, "Each day is going to get better. It may not seem like it at first, especially those first few days or even weeks after experiencing the loss, but it will get better day by day." God will restore your joy. Nothing will ever replace the child you lost. However, the love and comfort of God can give you peace. There is neither guilt nor shame on the days that you may experience pain and joy simultaneously! There were days when I just wanted to stay in bed and look at pictures and memories of my baby girl. One thing that also helped me through my healing process was speaking with a therapist during this period of grief. Losing a baby is a traumatic experience, and I believe it is important to share your emotions with an unbiased person who is also a professional. Going to a grief counselor helped me to express my emotions and begin a healing process. Counseling can be good because grief is something that happens to us without choice. The after-effects of grief can be really tough, but it is beyond our control. A therapist can also assist by giving you helpful and encouraging tips and tools—coping mechanisms—when you have experienced the loss of a baby. My therapist encouraged me to journal, talk, and connect with other women who experienced this type of loss. Journaling was a tool that helped me to express my emotions and not harbor sadness. I was able to use the tool of journaling to pray and talk to God. It was helpful—I felt that I was not alone. I strongly encourage seeking out a therapist who can help you heal during this experience. There are many stages of grief: denial, anger, bargaining, depression, and acceptance.[1] Grief counselors can help you start to recover from grief and renew your mind. They can help you consciously try to process the pain and choose to look toward the future. Focus on healing and self-care. I feel, especially in the African American communities, that going to a therapist is not really often talked about (there's a misconception here), but I feel it can be a very helpful and successful tool as everyone grieves differently. If our hair needs to be washed, we will go to a salon. If our teeth need cleaning, we go to a dentist. If our body is in pain, we go to a doctor, so why not care for our mental and emotional health by seeking the services of professionals. I feel mental health is just as important as our other needs—even if just for a few sessions. What helped me was finding a Christian, faith-based counselor who was medically licensed and also a minister. This allowed me to consult a licensed professional who also encouraged me with the word of God.

Allow yourself time to heal, but do not get stuck. I would do small things around the house that would bring me joy. For example, I enjoy taking bubble baths and warm showers. On days that I felt down, simple things such as a relaxing bubble bath would go a long way. I also invested in a diffuser, and I would use essential oils known to boost moods, such as lavender, ylang-ylang, frankincense, and lemongrass. Something as simple as going for a walk to get fresh air proved to be helpful. I enjoy shopping for home decor, candles, and makeup. Having a day or a few hours to take my mind off of my stresses and worries was helpful, so a small dose of retail therapy proved to be helpful from time to time.

One important thing, always remember that God has a perfect plan for you. I encourage you today to give yourself time to heal mentally, physically, spiritually, and emotionally. Do not push yourself too hard. Remember and understand that some things in life that happen are not in our control. This one was hard for me, and I tried desperately not to blame myself. Even with all the precautions mothers take during pregnancy, things can be totally out of our control. Trust God and know that He can heal you during your time of grief. "For I know the thoughts that I think toward you, saith the LORD, thoughts of peace, and not of evil, to give you an expected end" (Jeremiah 29:11 KJV).

I encourage you today to not get stuck in sadness, grief, or depression. Put all your trust in God, and pray daily for restoration. God can do all things! And you can do all things through Him. Use this time of grief to strengthen your time with God. I encourage you to pray, read the Word, journal with God, listen to uplifting sermons, go to church, and be encouraged by your church community. Journaling was a major tool that helped me pour my feelings out to God on paper. It allowed me to release my emotions. Also, by journaling, I can now reflect and look back at how God helped me overcome my grief and loss. Never forgotten, but able to move forward and find peace and happiness. Allow God to heal you as only He CAN!

As you are experiencing this time of grief, I encourage you to pray this prayer with me:

> *Father God, I thank you for this day, Lord. Lord, I praise Your holy name because You are worthy to be praised. Lord, I pray that you heal me during this time of grieving, Lord. Lord, I pray that You reveal my purpose in this pain that I am experiencing, Lord. Lord, your word says in Romans 8:28, "ALL things work together for the good of them that love the Lord and are*

called according to your purpose Jesus." Lord, I know that right now I am experiencing pain, Lord. Right now I am experiencing sadness, Lord but I pray that You heal me right now in the name of Jesus. Lord, I know that You are allowing me to go through this pain so that I can be a testimony to someone else so that You can get the glory. Lord, I pray right now in the name of Jesus that You heal my pain, Lord and restore my joy. God, allow me to press forward Jesus and be strong in You. Lord, I pray for a speedy recovery and healing in the name of Jesus. Send Your angels to protect my husband and me during this time of mourning, Lord God and restore us. Lord, I trust You and I honor You, and it's in the mighty name of Jesus I pray. Amen!"

Journal Prompt:

I encourage you to express your thoughts below by beginning to journal. How are you feeling at this moment? Then, think of one word that expresses how you feel today. What does the word mean to you, and why? Remember, journaling is a judgment-free place to express your emotions and explore your thoughts and feelings.

_____
_____
_____
_____
_____
_____
_____
_____
_____
_____
_____
_____
_____
_____
_____

Chapter Four

WALKING THROUGH GRIEF
Don't Blame Yourself, but Educate Yourself

After losing my baby, I went through a phase or a short period where I was blaming myself. As parents or soon-to-be parents, my husband and I immediately began preparing for our baby when we found out we were pregnant. And as parents, you always want the best for your child. Having experienced the loss of a child during pregnancy, you may go through a period where you blame yourself for the loss. In my mind, I would have thoughts of, "I wish I would have done this, or I wish I would have done that. Was it something that I ate, did not eat, or more I could have done?" For me, it was being diagnosed with preeclampsia, which came to me as a complete shock. Prior to my pregnancy, I had no clue what preeclampsia was. I truly believe women should educate themselves and be more aware of pregnancy complications, especially if they are diagnosed with preeclampsia or other medical conditions that can prove harmful to mother and child. According to the Preeclampsia Foundation, "preeclampsia is a condition unique to human pregnancy. It is diagnosed by the elevation of the expectant mother's blood pressure, usually after the 20th week of pregnancy. Most women with preeclampsia will deliver healthy babies and fully recover. However, some women will experience complications, several of which may be life-threatening to the mother and/or baby. A woman's condition can progress to severe preeclampsia very quickly. Most women with preeclampsia will deliver healthy babies and fully recover. However, some women will experience complications, several of which may be life-threatening to the mother and/or baby. The rate of preeclampsia in the US has increased 25% in the last two decades and is a leading cause of maternal and infant illness and death."[1]

The loss of our baby girl was devastating and traumatic. After being diagnosed with preeclampsia in my third trimester, I was referred to a perinatal specialist. At the initial perinatal appointment, my vitals were not in a range that warranted me being admitted to the hospital, but they were borderline. I never made it to the second follow-up specialist appointment because we lost our baby girl the day before I was scheduled to see the doctor again. This was devastating, and I would debate in my mind. I wish the doctor would have just admitted me on that Friday. Only if I had known what would happen. If you notice anything that feels off or different, you should never hesitate to contact your doctor. It is very important to stay consistent with your doctor appointments and follow-up appointments. If you have any questions or concerns, definitely discuss with your physician options for overnight observation. Be sure to contact your doctor if you are in any pain or experiencing unusual discomfort. Remember, you are the best advocate for your and your child's health.

Being in the hospital was traumatic. I remember not hearing my baby's heartbeat after arriving at the hospital via ambulance, and the doctors placing me on the fetal monitor. After having an emergency C-section, my baby girl Gia Teresa Russell was stillborn. The doctors were able to resuscitate her. However, due to the amount of oxygen lost to the brain she did not survive. It was determined that I suffered from a placenta abruption. This was my first pregnancy, and I did not know what to expect and was completely distraught after the loss.

After some time passed, I would think to myself about my health and healthcare options. I feel it is important to have conversations with your doctor(s) —especially after having suffered a prior miscarriage or stillbirth. It's important for your doctor and you to have a plan for another pregnancy to determine the best medical options based on your medical history. My OBGYN and I would later discuss a plan for my future pregnancies and decided that I would most likely be hospitalized and on bed rest if I developed preeclampsia or elevated blood pressure again. Unfortunately, conditions such as preeclampsia can be genetic, and there is nothing that you can do to prevent it. I highly recommend speaking with your physician on the best options for your health.

If you, too, are experiencing a period of blaming yourself, please don't! Instead of focusing your energy and thoughts on blame, reframe your mind to focus on educating yourself on what you can do to improve the state of your health going forward.

For me, I began to extensively research

preeclampsia. I didn't know what this was prior to being diagnosed a few days before I lost my baby. Especially after having a normal pregnancy up until about the 34-week mark. My diagnosis was shocking because I was never on medications or had any other medical conditions in my life before my pregnancy, especially related to high blood pressure. Unfortunately, it was genetic in my situation as my mother too developed preeclampsia during her pregnancy with me.

In general, we do not commonly speak about the risks and the importance of good health during pregnancy. This may be a bigger issue in Black communities, but there may be a lack of education overall related to prenatal health. According to the National Partnership for Women and Families, "Black women are three to four times more likely to experience pregnancy-related death than white women. Black women are more likely to experience preventable maternal death compared with white women. Black women's heightened risk of pregnancy-related death spans income and education levels."[2]

I feel it is very important to always constantly improve upon yourself. I stress the importance of educating yourself, not of a mindset of fear but one of preparation. For example, for me, during my pregnancy many things came to my surprise. For instance, morning sickness—I did not realize that morning sickness was not only just in the morning but any time of the day. I recall during my first pregnancy after working my 9-to-5, I was going through downtown Atlanta, bumper to bumper traffic, pregnant in my first trimester, and I suddenly felt the need to throw up. Sadly, I could not pull over my car fast enough due to the traffic, and I literally vomited in my lap in my car. It was terrible! Once I made it home, I remember my husband having to help me out and clean up the car. I tell this story to say that often no one glamorizes the "negative" aspects of pregnancy. From that one experience, I was always careful to keep a towel in my car in case of emergencies like this, and I always had snacks and water handy if I felt an urge to eat or became nauseous.

I also remember being in pain one night in my second trimester and feeling cramping sensations. I did not know what it was, and I called my doctor's office and spoke with a nurse who determined that I was experiencing Braxton Hicks contractions.

There were many changes to my body I experienced during my pregnancy, and one thing that I wanted to avoid was stretch marks early in my pregnancy. I conducted my research and decided to purchase coconut body oils and moisturizers that were suggested and touted as helpful in avoiding stretch marks during pregnancy as the skin on the stomach stretches to accommodate your child's growth. I also experienced changes in my breast and nipple size. PLEASE, never feel embarrassed to ask your doctor any questions that you have regarding your health. Ultimately, and amazingly, as women we endure so much to bring life into this world. It is very important that you seek an OBGYN that will be attentive to your needs. Use this time to revisit the doctor if you need to and discuss your concerns, your health, and pregnancy options in the future.

As women, post-pregnancy, our bodies go through a lot of different physical and hormonal changes. Depending on how far you are in your pregnancy can impact how much weight you may have gained and even different things such as your shoes, not fitting due to swollen feet. For me, one of the most difficult things I had to go through was extracting milk from my breast after losing my baby. This had both a psychological and physical impact on me. Everyone's experience can be different. Not all women experience lactation issues after a miscarriage or stillbirth.

During your stay in the hospital, a lactation consultant may discuss options for extracting milk and other things to do to make nursing more comfortable and successful. The process can be a little overwhelming, especially if you are faced with possibly losing your child or, like me, unable to nurse my baby because she was in the Neonatal Intensive Care Unit (NICU). I felt powerless and just wanted to do everything I could to save my child. Once I made it home from the hospital, I recall my breast being extremely sore and uncomfortable and trying to use a breast pump to relieve the milk. Take as much time as you need to determine the best option for you and your family regarding lactation. Some mothers may choose to donate their breast milk to a baby in need. I chose the option of lactation suppression. It also can be painful if someone simply hugs you tightly. I believe this process was one the most difficult because my breast were functioning, as they should have, to feed my baby, and dealing with self-extracting can be tough. What really helped me through this process and taught me how to stop my breasts from producing breast milk was speaking with a lactation consultant on how to stop the breast milk and reduce the pain. My grandmother advised me to use cabbage leaves, by placing them in my bra to help with lactation suppression. It seemed very odd to use cabbage, not to mention the awkward smell in my bra, but it definitely helped. I strongly recommend speaking with your OBGYN, nurse, family members, or friends on the various options. The use of cold compresses or gel packs also helps to reduce the pain.

Personally, after going through this, I learned the importance of taking responsibility for the things I can control and change, and the things I cannot control, and change, it does not help to worry and become obsessed about. Managing stress was a huge area I needed to improve in. After having gone through such a traumatic experience of losing my baby, amongst other things in life, I eventually learned that stressing does not solve problems. The Bible says in James 1:2-4 (NIV), "Consider it pure joy, my brothers and sisters, whenever you face trials of many kinds because you know that the testing of your faith produces perseverance. Let perseverance finish its work so that you may be mature and complete, not lacking anything." My interpretation of this scripture is that we, as believers, have to learn how to find some peace and joy in the midst of trials. Of course, this does not mean trying times in our lives are joyful or pleasurable but more so that it is the pruning of the tests and trials that develop us. If you focus on passing the test, then you will be able to finish the chapter and move on to the next test life has to offer. For instance, if we consider a loss or grief as a short, temporary period in our lives, we can think of it as passing a test. Instead of developing anger, rage, and resentment from grief, focus on becoming overcome with joy to pass the spiritual test.

Another huge scripture that helped me with this was in the book of Matthew. This really helped me put things into perspective. Do not worry about things. Be as worry-free as the birds. You never see a bird distraught and worrying about what it will eat, how will it provide for its babies, is it going to rain tomorrow, or what will it do? So, I feel that God is saying, "Don't I always provide for you as I have done for in the past?" It shows a true lack of faith when we worry and do not trust God.

Study Scriptures Matthew 6:25-34 (KJV):

25 "Therefore I tell you, do not worry about your life, what you will eat or drink; or about your body, what you will wear. Is not life more than food, and the body more than clothes?

26 Look at the birds of the air; they do not sow or reap or store away in barns, and yet your heavenly Father feeds them. Are you not much more valuable than they?

27 Can any one of you by worrying add a single hour to your life?

28 "And why do you worry about clothes? See how the flowers of the field grow. They do not labor or spin.

29 Yet I tell you that not even Solomon in all his splendor was dressed like one of these.

30 If that is how God clothes the grass of the field, which is here today and tomorrow is thrown into the fire, will he not much more clothe you—you of little faith?

31 So do not worry, saying, 'What shall we eat?' or 'What shall we drink?' or 'What shall we wear?'

32 For the pagans run after all these things, and your heavenly Father knows that you need them.

*33 But seek first his kingdom and his righteousness,
and all these things will be given to you as well.
34 Therefore do not worry about tomorrow, for
tomorrow will worry about itself."*

My husband really helped me to slowly get delivered from worrying and stress management. Especially when dealing with something stressful at work—that may have caused huge financial impacts, etc. I would talk to my husband about things that were worrisome and stressful. If you are facing something stressful in your life, it is always good to talk to a loved one or a friend just to gain a clearer perspective. When sharing stressful moments with my husband, I would often find that I could have just been overreacting to a situation or over-thinking it. For some reason, in general I think most men are more relaxed and laid back. I knew this was an area where my husband exhibited strength. He taught me various ways to deal with and approach stressful situations—with his calm, carefree demeanor. My mindset began to take a sudden shift whenever I felt stress creeping in. I learned to consider the following:

1. Is this within my control? If so, what can

I do to change the outcome? Take action! If not, definitely don't worry about it!
2. If it is out of my control, pray about it. Let go and Let God!

I encourage you to write these questions down and reflect on them as needed as you face day-to-day challenges. And remember, do not blame yourself! Despite how the situation may look or feel at the moment, God has a plan for your life. Use this time to pray, study, gain wisdom and insight, and strengthen your relationship with God through prayer and fasting.

Encouragement Prayer:

Jesus thank You for this day, God. I pray that you give me and my family the strength and guidance to heal during this time, Lord. God, I pray that You release me from any shame and guilt this experience may have placed on my heart. Lord, I trust that You will help restore me physically, mentally, and emotionally. God, I pray that You give me the tools and wisdom to help me through. Send Your angels of protection to help me during this time. Lord, I rebuke the spirit of fear and shame. Help me to be unashamed and to get the help that I need during this time. Lord, I thank you, and I pray all these prayers in Your son Jesus Christ's name. AMEN.

Below are scripture references that I hope you find helpful:

- "Wisdom and money can get you almost anything, but only wisdom can save your life" (Ecclesiastes 7:12 NLT).
- "Seek the LORD and his strength, seek his face continually" (1 Chronicles 16:11 KJV).
- "Do your best to present yourself to God as one approved, a worker who does not need to be ashamed and who correctly handles the word of truth" (2 Timothy 2:15 NIV).
- "If any of you lacks wisdom, you should ask God, who gives generously to all without finding fault, and it will be given to you" (James 1:5 NIV).
- "A wise man will hear, and will increase learning; and a man of understanding shall attain unto wise counsels" (Proverbs 1:5 KJV).

Journal Prompt:

I encourage you to take this time to write down a few things that are heavy on your heart and lay them at the feet of God.

_____
_____
_____
_____
_____
_____
_____
_____
_____
_____
_____
_____
_____
_____
_____
_____
_____
_____
_____

Chapter Five

PRIORITIZE YOUR HEALTH

I highly recommend that you consult with your trusted medical professional about options to improve your health. Once your doctor has cleared you to return to regular tasks and/or exercising. I feel it is very important to focus on improving your health. It does not matter your weight or size. There is always an opportunity to improve your health. What really helped me to lose the post-pregnancy weight and regain my stamina was spin class. I signed up with a gym that offered spin classes and other classes such as Barre, Total Resistance Exercises (TRX), etc. Of course, during the first month I started back exercising, I only did very light exercises. Becoming active helped me a great deal. It kept me focused on the positive and aided in moving forward. I had a routine, and around three months in, I could tell that I was losing weight, building strength, and increasing my stamina. Exercising also improves stress. According to Harvard Health, "Regular physical activity keeps you healthy and reduces stress."[1] I encourage you to get active when you can. However, it does not have to require anything expensive, such as a gym membership. Things such as walking in your neighborhood or with a group of friends, working out in your home by using online workout videos, or even deep cleaning your home can increase your activity.

I also recommend focusing on your diet. I know for me, especially if I am going through a trying period, it is so much easier to constantly reach for that ice cream in the fridge. I had to learn that when I am experiencing moments or grieving to not put my focus on comfort foods, but rather focus on laying my pain at the feet of God—praying, journaling, and fasting. I am not saying to not treat yourself, but rather focus on things you can do to improve your health related to your diet. I focused on drinking more water, eliminating certain foods such as pork and shellfish, and focusing on overall cleaner eating and less unhealthy fast foods.

You may want to also speak with your doctor

about which vitamins and supplements he/she recommends specifically for you.

Focus on improving your health, exercising, diet, and stress management. Just by doing these things, you are putting in the work! "Faith without works is dead" (James 2:26 KJV). If you trust that God will restore your health and provide you with a baby in the future or fulfill the desires of your heart, I think it is important that you meet Him halfway and let God do the rest. I believe it is unfair to expect God to provide, and you are not willing to do your part. Become more intimately connected to God, clean up your diet, exercise, reduce stress, and let God do the rest!

Pray this Prayer with me:

Lord God,

I repent of my sins. Wash me with the blood of Jesus. Lord, please renew my mind. Lord, I repent of any moment that I may have blamed myself and doubted You, God. Lord, I know that You have a perfect will for my life. Lord, I pray that You restore my health in the name of Jesus. Lord, I pray that You strengthen me in areas that I may be weak, God. I pray that You give me the energy and the strength to exercise more and to get healthier. Lord, I trust that You can do all things! Lord, please reveal to me the areas that I need to improve in my life— emotionally, spiritually, and physically. Lord, I pray that You heal my body; reveal to me anything that is not of You. Show the areas of my life that are not of You. Give me the ability, courage, and strength to eat healthy. Father God, show me the things that I need to eat to improve my diet. Lord, I ask that You will give me favor. Lord, I pray that You remove all stress, worry, and anxiety. I lay all cares at your feet. Lord Your Word says, "But they that wait upon the

LORD shall renew their strength; they shall mount up with wings as eagles; they shall run, and not be weary; and they shall walk, and not faint. (Isaiah 40:31 KJV)." I pray this in Your son Jesus Christ name. AMEN!

Journal Prompt:

What are some physical activities you enjoy? What is an exercise, fitness class, and/or activity that you have never tried and would like to try?

_____
_____
_____
_____
_____
_____
_____
_____
_____
_____
_____
_____
_____
_____
_____
_____
_____
_____

Chapter Six
DON'T BE AFRAID TO SHARE YOUR STORY

One of the main things that compelled me to write this book was the number of women, and even men, who opened up to me after my husband and I suffered our loss and shared that they or someone in their immediate family had suffered the loss of a baby due to miscarriage, stillbirth, or Sudden Infant Death Syndrome (SIDS). What pushed and propelled me to write this even more were the people in my family sharing that they too had gone through a miscarriage, stillbirth, etc. At this point, I knew if there were people in my own family that opening up to me, after the fact, there were even more people out there in the world who had similar experiences and may feel alone.

Let me say this again, "YOU ARE NOT ALONE." There is someone else out there that may be in your family or community that has gone through this as well! The enemy wants you to feel alone and that no one else has gone through this experience. I rebuke that spirit in the name of Jesus. The Bible says in Revelation 12:11 KJV, "And they overcame him by the blood of the Lamb, and by the word of their testimony; and they loved not their lives unto the death." I am now a strong believer that we should not be afraid to share our testimony. My personal prayer is if I can encourage just one person through sharing my testimony, I have fulfilled my purpose in writing this book. If you feel that God is leading you to encourage someone else, please do it. Obey God! There is great reward in obedience. You do not have to feel obligated to share every detail of your experience, but I encourage you to encourage someone else in your family, community, or church that may have suffered from a miscarriage or loss of an infant. I believe that along with prayer and strengthening my relationship with God, one thing that helped me to heal was different people sharing their stories with me—stories from co-workers, church members, family, and even my gym instructor sharing with me her personal experience from suffering a loss of a baby. My intention and purpose of this book is to help anyone avoid suffering in silence. For me, it was helpful sharing my story with others, and as I look back on it, it was a tremendous help in my healing process. I was also able to connect with others who experienced something similar to what I experienced. I encourage you to not feel neither ashamed nor fearful if you would like to share your story.

Many people may be ashamed to tell their stories because they feel they have no one to talk to or anyone who could relate. I encourage you to find someone in your community, social media group, etc.—just find someone to talk to and share your story. I remember a year after I experienced the loss of my baby, the hospital that I was taken to called me for an in-person interview on my experience and how they could learn and grow from me sharing my story. The director of the hospital's maternity department called me around the anniversary of my baby's death. I remember getting the call, and initially being skeptical because I literally feared going back to that hospital. I was afraid it would bring back so many terrible memories. I prayed about it and later talked to my husband about it, and we decided to do it together. The hospital's director and the entire maternity nursing team were present for my interview. There were roughly twenty-five people in the room. Overall, they asked me about my experience, and I gave them feedback on the things I could remember. One thing that I did give them feedback on was perhaps they could have made the final moments of our time with our baby more memorable. I felt they should have asked if there was anything special I wanted her to wear or be wrapped in during her final moments. I do, however, remember they called the Chaplain to come pray during the final moments. My husband was there with me during the interview, and the director was very passionate about hearing about his experience. One feedback my husband shared was during the chaos of it all, during the loss, many were focused on "mom" and "baby," and there was very little to no focus on the dad, who was also experiencing the trauma of losing a child and was charged with handling the arrangements. Fathers' stories are just as important as mothers'. Overall, I thought by sharing my story with the hospital staff, would hopefully help improve someone else's experience, and at least the hospital was willing to consider my feedback.

Ultimately, in the end, I did thank them for their service, their willingness to listen to not only my but my husband's journey while being cared for at their facility, and their consideration to improve where they can utilize the notes from our interview.

Regardless of what stage of pregnancy you were in or how young your baby was when you lost him/her, there is an immediate bond you have with your baby from the moment you hear the words, "You're pregnant." The Word says, "Before I formed thee in the belly I knew thee; and before thou camest forth out of the womb I sanctified thee, *and* I ordained thee a prophet unto the nations" (Jeremiah 1:5 KJV). If you suffered a miscarriage, depending on the stage of your pregnancy, you might not have been showing to others, but there was a baby. I am a firm believer that all babies go to Heaven and are with God. We can just pray that one day we will be reunited with them in Heaven.

Chapter Seven
RESTORATION

There was a period, maybe months, after the loss where I would have random days I just laid in the bed and cried. One day I came across the story of Naomi in the Bible, the book of Ruth. I related so much to this story. More specifically, when Naomi said that God changed her name to Mara, which means "bitter," to weep bitterly or grieve bitterly, strong chief waters (tears) in the Hebrew language. If you have not read the Book of Ruth, I encourage you to do so. For some reason, I really connected with this story. My connection was in how Naomi experienced the loss of loved ones. At a high level of the story, Naomi's husband and two sons passed away. I could not imagine going through this, but I know what it is like to lose loved ones. I related to Naomi in her period of grief and bitterness. There were times when I thought, "God, why did this happen to me?" I would see stories on the news where parents intentionally left their children in hot cars, and the child later died; or hear stories of people abandoning their babies. I could never imagine how a parent could intentionally harm their child. It would make me wonder how someone like this was allowed to become a parent, and I just lost my child prematurely through no fault of my own. But then I quickly remembered God's grace, knowing that all sin is sin in God's eyes. Everyone desires God's grace. I would try to remember that God would never leave me nor forsake me. Deuteronomy 31:6 (NIV) says, "Be strong and courageous. Do not be afraid or terrified because of them, for the LORD your God goes with you; he will never leave you nor forsake you." Just like in the story of Naomi in the Book of Ruth, God can restore the years of the cankerworm.

I was also encouraged by Joel 2:25-32 (KJV):

"25 And I will restore to you the years that the locust hath eaten, the cankerworm, and the caterpillar, and the palmerworm, my great army which I sent among you.

26 And ye shall eat in plenty, and be satisfied, and praise the name of the Lord your God, that hath dealt wondrously with you: and my people shall never be ashamed.

27 And ye shall know that I am in the midst of Israel and that I am the Lord your God, and none else: and my people shall never be ashamed.

28 And it shall come to pass afterward, that I will pour out my spirit upon all flesh; and your sons and your daughters shall prophesy, your old men shall dream dreams, your young men shall see visions:

29 And also upon the servants and upon the handmaids in those days will I pour out my spirit.

30 And I will shew wonders in the heavens and in the earth, blood, and fire, and pillars of smoke.

31 The sun shall be turned into darkness, and the

> *moon into blood, before the great and terrible day of the Lord come.*
>
> *32 And it shall come to pass, that whosoever shall call on the name of the Lord shall be delivered: for in mount Zion and in Jerusalem shall be deliverance, as the Lord hath said, and in the remnant whom the Lord shall call."*

I interpret these scriptures as: God will restore me just as He did Israel. Anything that the enemy has tried to destroy God can restore it. So, hold your head up and have hope! It may not seem like it right now, but God can restore your "locust years." When I say "locust years," I mean that painful time period or grief loss or sorrow. God can restore your lost years you by deepening your relationship with Christ."

This period of grief is just a short season in your life. You have to have faith that God will restore you and fulfill His purpose through you. At times, the weight of loss and grief can be so heavy, but that is the reason we believe. I believe metaphorically that faith is the currency of the Kingdom of Heaven.

What does the bible say about faith? "For as the body without the spirit is dead, so faith without works is dead also" (James 2:26 KJV). Mark 11:24 KJV says, "Therefore I say unto you, What things soever ye desire, when ye pray, believe that ye receive them, and ye shall have them. Whatever you say, speak and trust God for you shall have." This helped me to build my confidence in God. I trusted that God allowed this to happen for a reason. Was it to bring me closer to Him? Was it not my timing to have a child on this Earth? Was it to protect me from something that may have happened to my baby in the future that I may not and could not have handled? I am not sure. I cannot answer these questions, but I began to lean on God to be grateful for what I did have. I could have died during childbirth. I could have lost my state of mind. I begin to thank God for my husband—who loves me. I thanked God for my family and my home and for being surrounded by love. I just trusted that in this season, I am supposed to enjoy this time with my husband and enjoy him, serve, and submit to him as though to Christ. I focused on building my marriage and loving on my husband. In God's timing, He will fulfill our hearts' desires. I started to thank God for the things that I did have.

So, back to the story of Naomi. After Naomi's loss of her husband and two sons, all that remained were her daughters-in-law, Orpah and Ruth. In the end, God completely restored her. She was used by God to help Ruth marry Boaz and later had grandchildren and was one of the ancestors of King David. Despite Naomi's losses, she did not give up. She kept her faith and poured love into her daughter-in-law, Ruth, and was blessed in her later days. Just like Naomi, God can restore you.

Whenever you are facing grief, sorrow, or bitterness, call upon the Lord God. Pray for strength. Pray this prayer with me:

Lord,

>*I don't know why You allowed this to happen to me, but I know that Your Word says that You will never leave me or forsake me. You are my rock and my strength. God, please give me the strength to carry on. Give me the strength to move past the grief, Lord God. Restore my joy, restore my strength, restore my happiness. I will not be defeated in the name of Jesus. Lord, I know that You have a perfect plan for my life, I*

may not understand it or I may have made some decisions that were not Your will, but God, I repent. I have faith that in due season You will restore my life. I pray that I fulfill my purpose on this Earth and let Your will be done. In Your son Jesus's name Amen.

Journal Prompt:

If you so feel led, I encourage you to write down some of the emotions you are feeling. Also, what are some things, no matter how big or small, you feel you are hopeful for in the future?

_____
_____
_____
_____
_____
_____
_____
_____
_____
_____
_____
_____
_____
_____
_____
_____
_____
_____

Chapter Eight

THE AFTERMATH

It is such a harsh reality to face grieving after losing a baby through stillbirth—or at all. For us, one of the harsh realities was coming back home from the hospital and having a fully decorated nursery with no baby. I was so excited about decorating the nursery throughout our pregnancy. I remember my husband putting up pink butterflies in the baby's nursery near her changing table. I also have many great memories of my in-laws coming over to our home and helping us hang paintings. One special gift my mother-in-law gave me was a reframing of a piece of custom stitched artwork my mother gifted me when I was a baby. She had it reframed in a pink and white, modern design. It is with great excitement as I remember my husband and father-in-law installing the chandelier in the baby's nursery. We hung up each crystal; it was so beautiful. I also remember my father throwing me two beautiful baby showers. I was showered with gifts, love, food, and family. Both of our families were so happy. This would be the first grandchild for both of our parents. I remember going with family members to register for the baby items, and one of my favorite stores was Pottery Barn. Our families purchased every single item on our registry. We were so blessed and grateful. Memories like this I will always cherish—priceless.

I just remember being on "cloud nine" with a nursery full of onesies, diapers, wipes, bottles, baby books, and more. One of my favorite gifts was a pink faux mink coat that my aunt purchased for the baby. It was so adorable. After sitting in awe of all our gifts and writing thank you cards, I would not have known or imagined that within two weeks, we would lose our baby girl, Gia.

I wish I could turn back the hands of time and go back to my last doctor's appointment. I wish that they would have just admitted me to the hospital instead of sending me home, but there is nothing I can do but move forward and trust that God has a perfect plan.

It was hard for me to breakdown the nursery. I didn't start this process until about six months after our loss. I say that to say, no one should force you to get rid of items or put away things. This should be a decision between you and your husband. One thing that helped me to start was by gifting the items. I connected with a co-worker who shared that her daughter had experienced a miscarriage with her first pregnancy years prior, and I was happy to hear that she was expecting a baby boy. I remember taking a car full of our gender-neutral items that she could use, such as wipes, diapers, newborn laundry detergent, etc. She was extremely appreciative, and I felt good donating my baby's items to someone I knew. Also, with unpacking your nursery, it's good to have mental support. It may be rough emotionally going through items and boxing them. I was grateful for my mother-in-law, who helped me go through the clothes and donate them to charity.

I decided to keep most of our major items, such as the crib, rocking chair, stroller, diaper pail, etc. There were also a few clothing items that were sentimental gifts that we kept. By keeping the things, we can use in the future was an act of faith. We were trusting God that in His perfect timing, He would bless us again.

Chapter Nine

HAVING THE FAITH TO MOVE FORWARD

In order to try to gain the strength to move forward, you may need some type of closure. Losing a baby is not something you will never forget. However, you can gain strength and the faith to press forward. There is not a day that does not go by that I do not think about my baby girl, but God has given me the strength to carry on. For some, it may be too tough to move forward emotionally without some type of event to signify that the mourning phase is over. For instance, some people may want to have a balloon release, funeral, write a letter to their baby, have a small ceremony, or some may not want to do anything at all. This is your and your spouse's decision, and do not feel obligated or pressured to do something that you do not want to do. You may also want to join an organized support group of women who may have lost their babies as well. But again, everyone is different. You have the right to decide what is best for you and your family.

You may begin to question, "How long will I feel this way?" There is no one answer, and this can vary by person. The length of your pregnancy does not determine the impact. You may have been pregnant for one day, or longer this does not matter in regards to how long you may mourn. Don't compare yourself to what others may have done. Use this time to talk about the loss with your spouse. For me, I found that journaling was the beginning phase to help me to move forward. Whereas for my husband, I found that he decided to pour himself into expanding his business and entrepreneurship as a coping mechanism. You may find that you want to work more to allow this to occupy your mind rather than focus on the grief and sorrow. It took me several months before I was focused on work. My husband encouraged me to open a business. By starting a new online boutique, I was able to find a hobby that I enjoyed, which was fashion, and it allowed me to put my energy into something that was a hobby and did not feel like work. I was able to go to fashion shows, markets, and purchase wholesale clothing and jewelry. I found a lot of joy doing this, and now that I reflect on it, this helped me move forward and not be so stuck and sinking in sorrow. It was also nice to have some extra cash from the new business. For you, it may be something different. Think about the hobbies you enjoyed as a child or something that you enjoy doing even if you were not paid to do it. This may be painting, baking, horseback riding, swimming, or even volunteering with a local charity. I encourage you to find something that you enjoy when the time is right and put your energy into a hobby that you really enjoy—you never know where it will take you.

Once you begin to focus on these areas, it's important that you do not overwork or overexert yourself. Recognize when you need to rest physically, mentally, and emotionally. We lost our baby in early November (2018), close to the holiday season. I remember we were not up for going anywhere for large family gatherings, and it was okay. You do not have to put on a facade or a fake smile— especially if you feel it is too soon to attend certain events— just try not to remain in isolation too long.

When the time is right, you may want to speak with your physician about options to get pregnant again. How soon you want to pursue this journey may depend on how you feel mentally, emotionally, and physically.

Just because you faced this traumatic loss does not mean your life is over. You are still here on Earth because God has called you to complete a mission. If you don't know already, spend time with God and find out your purpose. Remember, pain is not our purpose. Too often, we mistake our pain as the ultimate purpose God has for our lives. Everything happens for a reason, and God will allow things in His timing. The Word of God says, "A man's heart plans his way, But the LORD directs his steps" (Proverbs 16:9 NKJV). As humans, we have plans and desires, but God has a perfect plan for our lives and will direct our steps. Perhaps God wants you to focus on another area in your life. Does he want you to get more involved in your church? Is there a new career that you need to seek? Is he calling you to get your finances in order? Know that these things can never replace what you have lost nor cover up how you are feeling. However, spend this time focusing on what you think God is calling you to do in this season.

By reading this book, I hope that you are encouraged and know that you are not alone. After facing this tragic loss in 2018, God restored my husband and me, and two years later we were able to get pregnant and have a HEALTHY, BOUNCING baby boy! I share this as encouragement—not to boast or brag but to give hope—if God can do it for me, He can also do it for you. God is all-powerful (omnipotent), all-knowing (omniscient), and all-present (omnipresent), and there are no limits to what He can do. The Word of God says in 2 Chronicles 7:14 KJV, "If my people, which are called by my name, shall humble themselves, and pray, and seek my face, and turn from their wicked ways; then will I hear from Heaven, and will forgive their sin, and will heal their land." After facing the loss, I prayed to God that He would restore my womb. I asked God to forgive me of all my sins and show me my ways that were not His ways.

SPECIAL MESSAGE

Disclaimer: This last chapter intends to give hope and inspiration to those who may be seeking to have a child after experiencing a loss.

Chapter Ten

GOD IS MY STRENGTH

In October 2019, we found out we were pregnant. I was so excited and nervous at the same time! I remember taking an at-home pregnancy test, and being so excited that it came back positive. The first doctor's appointment was nerve-racking because my husband and I were anxious to confirm our second pregnancy. I recall being so happy. I couldn't contain my little self. I wanted to share the news with everyone. My husband and I decided to share the news with our family, immediately. I am aware that some people wait until a later stage in their pregnancy to announce, especially if they have experienced a loss. For me, I wanted to shout to the world because

I was so happy! I knew in my heart that God would keep His promise to me, and we would have a healthy baby. I told my co-workers, and they were very happy for me! Some remarked that I was sharing the news too early as they knew my previous experience, but I did not care because I knew what God promised. Also, after sharing with my family, I found out that my first cousin was also expecting! It is so interesting how God works because we found out that we had the exact same due date—July 23, 2021. It was so good to have a family member to chat with along our pregnancy journey.

As the weeks went by, I would become nervous during my doctor's appointments. I just wanted everything to be fine with the baby. Sometimes I would get nervous during doctor's appointments because I would recall those memories of our first pregnancy. I would literally have to read a Bible verse or pray to calm down and focus on God in the moments that I would think about the previous experience during my doctor's appointments.

During my second pregnancy, I remember a pastor at my church giving me advice. She knew that I loved wearing heels every Sunday to church, and she recommended that I wear flats because heels may cause pressure on the uterus. I had never heard this before, but I was sure to wear flats or sneakers from that day on. Not that I would wear high heels every day, just occasionally. I say this to say if you have experienced a "public" loss, many offer you unsolicited advice, even if you do not ask for it. I knew that this advice and advice from other women meant well, but I always made the best decision for myself and consulted with my doctor if I had any questions.

I was happy that I was starting my pregnancy at a healthy weight based on my height. Those previous spin classes paid off. After I found out we were pregnant, I decided not to continue taking the spin class but opted just to do daily walks and pregnancy workout videos. One of co-workers gave me a pregnancy workout video that was very helpful. Always consult with your physician on the best options for you.

Fast forward to March 11, 2020. The day that the World Health Organization (WHO) declared Coronavirus (COVID-19) a global pandemic, it seemed like the world came to a screeching halt. When the United States declared a national state of emergency, it was surreal because many did not even know what COVID-19 was. Where did it come from? How did it spread? How deadly is it? According to the Centers for Disease Control and Prevention, "COVID-19 was identified in Wuhan, China in December 2019. COVID-19 is caused by the virus severe acute respiratory syndrome coronavirus 2 (SARS-CoV-2), a new virus in humans causing respiratory illness which can be spread from person-to-person. Early on in the outbreak, many patients were reported to be linked to a large seafood and live animal market. However, later cases with no link to the market confirmed person-to-person transmission of the disease. Additionally, travel-related exportation of cases has occurred."[1]

When the news began to spread about the virus, grocery stores immediately became crowded, and shelves became empty. I remember early during the outbreak going to the grocery store around 5:00 a.m. to get groceries and having to wait in a line that was over a thirty-minute wait. People were stocking up on food, water, and non-perishables. Many stores begin to run out of essential items.

During this time, I was in my second trimester, around the 23rd week of pregnancy. During one of my prenatal checkups with my OBGYN, she expressed concern for my health and safety during this time. She provided me with a note to work from home as there were no available studies on the impacts of COVID-19 on pregnant mothers and their unborn babies. Working from home was a blessing. It was also less stressful mentally having to deal with a daily commute and the physical impact on my body.

A few months passed, and it was now May 11th. I will never forget that date. Because of the COVID-19 pandemic, no guests could accompany me to my ultrasound appointments—not even my spouse. So, at this specific appointment, I was alone. I was going in for a routine prenatal appointment, and during the ultrasound, I could tell that the space around my baby's face in the ultrasound picture looked tight. The nurse took my blood pressure, and it was slightly elevated. At that point I became nervous as well. My doctor said I will have you admitted to the hospital because your amniotic fluid is a little low. At that moment, all of these memories of the first experience I had popped up. Based on my medical history of the first pregnancy, it was best for me to be admitted to be monitored as a safety precaution. At the time that I was admitted to the hospital, I was around 30 weeks pregnant. Let me tell you, the first day or so of being in the hospital was the worst. I was afraid and had such a traumatic first pregnancy, it was very hard to cast those fears down with this pregnancy. The plan was for the doctors to monitor my fluid levels and at least get me to my 34th week of pregnancy.

I remember being alone in the hospital room the first day, just praying that God would heal my baby. Because of the pandemic, no visitors or family members could come to see me in the hospital, only my spouse. I began to research things that I could do to increase my amniotic fluid, but unfortunately, there was nothing that I could do. My doctors simply recommended that I continue to drink water and remain on bed rest. My husband was able to visit me in the hospital and be with me. We would also talk a lot on the phone on the days he had to work. I remember the hospital room that I was in. The window was facing a brick wall. It was so discouraging to look out at that brick wall every day. One of the kind nurses felt my sorrow, and she advised me that she had put in a request to have my room changed to a better view. That was a very small thing that would later make a big difference.

Also, due to the pandemic, all of the hospital patients in the prenatal section could not leave their rooms unless they were going for an ultrasound or some other testing. It was very depressing mentally to not be able to leave the room. During this time, I had to really pray, journal, and depend on God.

As the days passed, different doctors would come in daily to give their analyses. I remember one doctor telling me that he did not think I would make it to the 34th week of pregnancy. The devil is a lie! Thankfully my trust was in God and not in man.

As time progressed, my fluid levels stabilized and became normal. Being on bed rest was very good for the baby and me. Even though my fluid levels were normal, my doctors decided to keep me on bed rest (in the hospital) until the baby arrived. But thankfully, all glory to God, I passed the 34th week of pregnancy, and things began to look even more hopeful. At 34 weeks, the pregnancy studies showed that babies' lungs were fairly well-developed. I was about to move to a new room at the hospital with a much better view. My co-workers were so supportive. They sent flowers and chocolates. My mother-in-law also sent balloons, flowers, candy, books, and encouraging, supportive notes.

All the sentiments from family and friends were greatly appreciated, kind-hearted, and encouraged me. My little sisters, family members and friends would talk to me daily (24/7) while they were on summer break. I decided to tell my immediate family that I did not want extended family and friends to know I was in the hospital. I knew no one could not come visit due to the pandemic, and I did not want anything posted on social media until after we had the baby. After experiencing a loss, everyone may be different as it relates to having a baby shower or what they would like to post to social media or share with family and friends. To help the time go by, I would journal and pray. It's funny how when we do not make time for God, He will sit us down to stop all the day-to-day commotion to focus on quality time with Him. Journaling, praising, worshiping, and worship music were all a part of my daily routine. The nurses commented on how pleasant I was as a patient. It appears that one would be surprised how many patients come to the hospital and feel a sense of entitlement and lack of respect for the staff.

In my hospital room, on the patient dry erase board, the nurse made a cute section for countdown days until the arrival of our baby boy. My husband came to the hospital and set up a maternity photoshoot for me with his camera. We used a sheet as a backdrop and then photoshopped the photos. After completing the editing, he made it look as if I was in a field of sunflowers. From the photos, you could not tell that I was in the hospital. That was another very happy and beautiful memory. Also, on the weekends and days that he did not have to work, my husband would bring me takeout. I already enjoy eating, but while I was pregnant, I really had a huge appetite and cravings. So he would bring me food from the Cheesecake Factory (one of my favorites) and other restaurants. I enjoyed hibachi, pasta, and the list goes on. I was definitely getting the "works" and enjoyed every moment of the third trimester—as much as I could.

Overall, the time in the hospital taught me patience and the importance of spending time with God. Which I had already known, but I learned to become more intentional about spending time with Him.

The night before our scheduled C-section, I was so excited! The morning of, I put on eyelashes and light makeup. I enjoy makeup, so it made me feel good by applying it before the delivery. That day it was just my husband and me. We went down to the prep area before the delivery, and I was so anxious and excited to know that my world would forever be changed. Our healthy baby boy, Ethan Omar Russell, arrived on July 2, 2020 at 7:45 a.m. We named him Ethan, a name of Hebrew origin meaning "firm, enduring, strong and long-lived."

God is a healer (Jehovah Rapha), and He is a promise keeper—faithful to answer ALL our prayers. God kept our baby and me healthy despite the challenges and unprecedented time of having a baby during a world pandemic. Looking back at it now, it may have been a blessing in disguise of the timing we had our baby because I had four months of maternity leave, and I also spent every day at home with him upon my return to work because I was working from home due to the pandemic. God is a promise keeper. In every situation, I try to always look for a bright side. By sharing my story with you, I hope you feel empowered and encouraged to never give up. Keep the faith! God will never leave you nor forsake you. It's no secret what God has done for others—He can do the same thing for you.

In conclusion, I would like to close this book with a prayer. If you are so led, please use this prayer and journal section to pour out your heart to God:

Prayer:

Father God,

I thank You for this day. Lord, I praise Your Holy name; You are worthy to be praised. Lord God, I pray that You help me and give me the strength to move forward. Lord, Your Word says that if we take delight in You that You would give us the desires of our hearts. Lord God, if You have called me to be a parent, I pray that You will help this come to pass. Lord, I pray against any ailment that is in my body or my spouse's body that may be causing us to miscarry. Lord, I pray against any demonic attack against us and our future child(ren) if You have called us to be parents. Lord God, in the name of Jesus, I repent of my sins. (Pray out loud for sins you may have committed). Lord, please forgive me of any known and unknown sins committed in my bloodline. Lord God, You are my healer and my redeemer. I pray that Your perfect will for my life be fulfilled. Lord, I pray that You reveal my purpose to me and help me to walk in my purpose. God, help me to get through this season in my life and restore my joy as only You can. I pray all of these prayers in your son Jesus Christ's name. AMEN!

Journal Prompt:

God wants you to cast your cares on Him (1 Peter 5:7 KJV).

Consider the following statements to assist with a jump-start conversation with God. List a Bible verse or song lyrics that uplift you, and note how you feel.
I am grateful for…
My prayer for today is…

_____
_____
_____
_____
_____
_____
_____
_____
_____
_____
_____
_____

ACKNOWLEDGMENTS

Dear God, thank you for giving me the strength and knowledge to write this book. My prayer is that this book reaches the eyes and ears of those whom You have intended for it to reach and to provide light, hope, comfort, and healing.

This book would not have happened without the support of my husband, Omar Russell. "I love you dearly."

Special thank you to Jennifer Stimson, who designed the beautiful book cover. To Dr. Jacqueline Walters, "Thank you for your diligent care and for writing the foreword." I am forever grateful to the developmental editorial assistance of Karolyne Roberts and Victoria Johnson for the earlier drafts and to my mother-in-law, Tonya Russell, for the later editorial drafts. Thank you all for pushing me to take my work to the next level.

To my grandparents, John and Verdis Richey, the late Calvin Ray Sr. and Betty Ray, my parents, Antonio and the late Francis Teresa Ray, my aunt,

Regina Ray, my cousin, Dr. Marilyn Carter, Prophetess Elaine Brunson, and my family, a special thank you for your continued prayers, encouragement, love and support. To all the women and men who shared their stories with me, "I thank you."

ABOUT THE AUTHOR

Author Photo by Kevin Goolsby

Shanease Russell is a follower of Jesus Christ, a wife, and a mother. Her mission is to help others heal and build their relationship with God. Shanease is a native of Atlanta, Georgia, and has a BS from Georgia State University.

"After my husband and I experienced the tragic loss of our baby, I was inspired to write this book to share my story with the hopes that it will help someone through their healing process and also show how God's love will help overcome such a loss. During the immediate days of our loss, the burden was heavy and overwhelming. My prayer is that this book will silence the shame of pregnancy loss and inspire other women to encourage others by sharing their stories. I truly hope my story inspires others to keep the faith." - Shanease Russell

Join "The Faith Within Circle" for support, encouragement, prayer or to connect with others who have been impacted miscarriage, stillbirth or infant loss visit the website at **www.thefaithwithin.com**.

To connect with Shanease, please visit her website at **www.shanease.com**. You can also follow her on social media at:

instagram.com/ShaneaseRussell
facebook.com/ShaneaseRussell
twitter.com/ShaneaseRussell

REFERENCES

1. MY STORY

1. Mostafavi, Beata. "Understanding Racial Disparities for Women with Uterine Fibroids." Weblog. 12 Aug. 2020. labblog.uofmhealth.org. 15 Oct. 2021. https://labblog.uofmhealth.org/rounds/understanding-racial-disparities-for-women-uterine-fibroids
2. Kriese, Rebecca. "The Creative Power of the Uterus and its Link to Uterine Fibroid." Weblog. Ayuseva.com. 16 Oct. 2021. https://www.ayuseva.com/wp-content/uploads/2013/11/The-Creative-Power-of-the-Uterus-and-its-link-to-Uterine-Fibroids.pdf
3. Preeclampsia Foundation. "What Is Preeclampsia." Weblog. 03 Aug 2021. Preeclampsia.org 16 Oct. 2021. https://www. preeclampsia.org/what-is-preeclampsia

2. YOU ARE NOT ALONE

1. Centers for Disease Control and Prevention. "Pregnancy and Infant Loss." 13 Aug. 2020. cdc.gov 4 Nov. 2021. https://www.cdc.gov/ncbddd/stillbirth/features/pregnancy-infant-loss.html

3. HEALING IN THE PROCESS

1. Kessler, David. "The Five Stages of Grief." Weblog. Grief.com. 16 Oct. 2021. https://grief.com/the-five-stages- of-

grief/

4. WALKING THROUGH GRIEF

1. Preeclampsia Foundation. "FAQs." Weblog. 17 Jan. 2020 PreeclampsiaFoundation.org 18 Sep. 2021. https://www.preeclampsia.org/faqs
2. National Partnership. "Black Women's Maternal Health: A Multifaceted Approach to Addressing Persistent and Dire Health Disparities." Weblog. 01 Apr. 2018 NationalPartnership.org. 12 Aug. 2021 https://www.nationalpartnership.org/our-work/health/reports/black-womens-maternal-health.html

5. PRIORITIZE YOUR HEALTH

1. Harvard Health Publishing. "The secret to better health – exercise." Weblog. 06 Mar. 2012. Harvard Medical School. 02 Nov.2021. https://www.health.harvard.edu/healthbeat/the-secret-to-better-health-exercise

10. GOD IS MY STRENGTH

1. Centers for Disease Control and Prevention. "COVID-19 Overview and Infection Prevention and Control Priorities in non-US Healthcare Settings." 26 Feb. 2021. cdc.gov. 16 Oct. 2021. https://www.cdc.gov/coronavirus/2019-ncov/hcp/non-us-settings/overview/index.html#background

Milton Keynes UK
Ingram Content Group UK Ltd.
UKHW021814260724
1052UKWH00025BA/71